Software Booklet: How to Become a 10X Developer

Florentin Bota

softwarebooklet.com

Software Booklet: How to Become a 10X Developer

Florentin Bota

softwarebooklet.com

Software Booklet: How to Become a 10X Developer

Florentin Bota

Published by:
Florentin Bota
Plopilor 73, ap. 1A, Cluj-Napoca,
Cluj, 400383 , Romania

ISBN: 979-8-7318-6062-8

Dedicated to

My colleagues at CodexWorks

&

To my students at

Babeș–Bolyai University

CONTENTS

INTRODUCTION

About the WHY

Let me tell you a story: A few years ago we were stuck on a feature that my colleagues have been working on for about a month and it would still have issues. Basically we were in development hell, pretty hard times, at that point we were almost sleeping at the office trying to make it work.

That project reached over half a million euros in value over time, but of course, at that specific point, it did not work and let's just say it did not feel great for us.

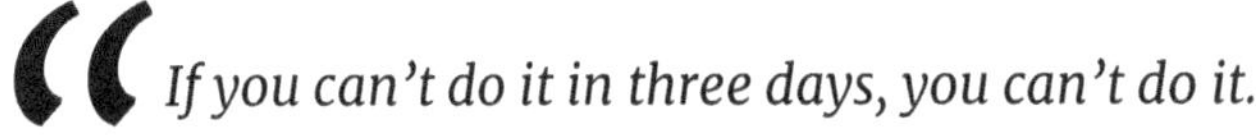 *If you can't do it in three days, you can't do it.*

You see, our first mistake was that we did not recognize the obvious rabbit hole we entered until it was too late. When this happens, the sooner you cut your losses, the better.

The quote above actually comes from my colleague George Monda, our CTO and I found it very useful in similar situations, especially with our more junior developers. Recognize when you are stuck and move along, ask for help or pivot/delegate.

So what happened, at first we decided that we should stop what we were doing (basically cascading changes) and then, **during a single night** I implemented the feature.

It worked and more than that, it worked for more than three years, until the process changed. Now the question is:

Was I **10** times more productive than my colleagues or not?

I like to think about it, maybe I was lucky, maybe I saw the problem from a different angle or maybe it just happened.

The thing is, I had a talk with my friend Gh. Vali after a few months and I told him that we need more people in our team. We started to figure it out and we realized we couldn't do it by ourselves. I jokingly said that we need a 10X developer so we can move things forward faster.

Vali said that most likely we already have a 10X dev in our team and I was starting to think a bit about myself, my colleagues… which one?

He was referring to me but I did not accept that label, maybe because I was not that confident in my skills at that point, or it just felt too silly for me.

I will discuss in this book exactly what the 10X development is, so hop along and let me tell you some more.

What I realized then is that we are all 10X developers, but not all the time. Funny, right?

I noticed that we have these spikes in productivity, we have moments, we have hours or maybe days when we will be extremely productive, you will get s*** done, and then… nothing.

You will look for energy everywhere but you will not find it and that's it, end of story. Or is it?

That's the thing, how can we increase our energy, how can we be more productive as developers, without burnout, without getting overworked?

The answer is very simple and it took me a while to get it. I do not wish to give spoilers in the introduction, but I guarantee that if you read this booklet you'll understand what it takes to be a better developer in a short amount of time.

There are a lot of troubles in our industry and that includes burnout, as I said before, there's a lot of stress, there's a lot of responsibility and between all that and all the meetings and all the discussions and all the architecture and all the bugs, we have to implement more features than ever.

Sometimes we lose that energy, we lose the drive, what I call the hunger mentality, when you are eager to learn, to create as much as possible, when you want to build applications and you really enjoy doing it.

Sometimes that energy dries up and you find it difficult to wake up in the morning, turn on your computer and start programming.

In this book, we'll discuss why this happens and what is needed to stop it. Just a teaser for now:

Let me tell you another story: This is about a company which hired a developer to help them solve an issue that bugged them

for over a year. They had some problems with a core functionality which was very, very hard to do (and by some it was impossible) so they found this developer who accepted the challenge.

This guy comes in at the office (yeah, this happened way before the pandemic), takes a seat and starts staring at the ceiling. He was thinking about the solution, how it would work. Of course, he had a deadline, it was about 2 months.

During the first day he was calm and continued to stare at the ceiling. The other colleagues were looking at him and at one point they asked: Are you okay?

He said he's solving the problem and, sure enough, he did not write a single line of code that day. The app was a monolith so it was kind of natural that they were looking with suspicion at their new colleague.

And yet, he came every day, took a seat at the office and stared at the ceiling with his hands under his head.

That continued for several weeks, and at one point, there was about one week remaining until the deadline and he came, took his seat and started looking again at the ceiling. Then he said: I got it!

That's when he started writing the code and **in one week he finished the whole application and it worked!** I ask you again:

Was he a 10X developer then ?

If so, was he a 10X developer in all the other weeks when he did not write a single line of code?

Once again, read this booklet and I promise you that you will understand what happened and how you can do it too.

Best, Florentin!

CHAPTER I

PRODUCTIVITY

The 10X developer is not a MYTH

Okay, so let's discuss productivity. I will dive straight into the subject 'cause I find it important to just get to the point.

People work differently and most importantly, their outputs are different.

There is this famous example where if you have 10 developers and you give them the same problem, you'll get 10 different results, 10 different programs. It is perfectly true.

In this regard, the specifications, ideally the technical specifications, help. So we will get the expected results, but people are still different and they will have different outputs.

So once again, coming back to productivity, what would that mean?

It's pretty simple, actually. Productivity refers to the actual output. What you give to others, so basically the utility that your work provides.

And now I would question, what is the utility? This is actually a term I learned while I was working on my PhD thesis.

It's an economics concept and refers to the total satisfaction that occurs when others consume your product or service.

Productivity is your output to the world

We can infer that until you get **some** output, it does not matter what you are doing. The results are what happens in the real world, outside of your own head. Shocking, right? Yet it makes perfect sense.

Regarding developers, there are two schools of thought. The first says that developers that are much more productive (10X is the used term for some reason) do not exist (myth) and that in real-life applications one cannot be proven to actually be more productive, in a controlled manner.

I would add just one thing to this: software managers know really well what a productive developer looks like. Indeed, it is not a controllable parameter, yet the differences between a slower developer and a great developer are visible to the naked eye.

One of the reasons I started writing this book was the words of my friend Adrian Lupau:

A senior will out-produce 10 juniors

Of course, it depends on the senior and the juniors, yet he is right. There are massive differences between what a beginner can do in a month and what a more experienced developer can build.

At the same time, a senior developer in a multi-national company might spend several days on a small feature, while a startup programmer will build a whole application in the same amount of time. Interesting!

So, to summarize... a 10X developer will develop code in 1/10th of the time, usually writing less code than the average developer.

The discussion is long and to put it shortly, 10X developers are considered by some the leprechauns of software engineering (really, there's a book about that).

We are at a point where the expectations we get as developers are usually not realistic and would require the said leprechaun to have them done.

What is even worse, once you start being really productive, the bar rises and people start expecting more and more from you, which is not that great actually.

Back to the origin: How the whole 10X story started?

In 1977, two software engineers conducted *"The Coding War Games"*, where 600 developers from dozens of companies competed in a productivity survey with programming challenges.

In their results, they observed about a 10X speed difference between the worst and the best teams. (11.1 times faster to be exact).

Also, the faster teams had better code quality and the programming language did not matter, except for Assembly (which makes sense).

Once again, this study does not prove that much. There are so many variables, like the team composition, experience, work style, communication etc, that it would not be fair to call this the start of the 10X concept.

Still, 10X developers, rock-star developers and unicorns are really sought after by startups to increase their chances of succeeding with their product.

I will be honest with you. We can all be 10X developers. You can be a 10X developer. Just remember to **compare the improvement with ourselves**.

There is a fallacy that we should compare with our more senior colleagues or some other teams that created Facebook, Apple or Microsoft in a garage.

Stop it, this will only hurt you in the long run. Look behind. Are you a better developer than you were 2 years ago?

Yes? Great!

Do the same for the next 2 years and you will be 10X better and 10X faster than you were to begin with.

No? Also great!

You should start improving your skills. Allocate 10 hours per week and build something that makes you proud.

Too busy to do it?

Create a team around your idea and let them help you build it. Software development is so much more than writing code. It is about building value for others.

Seth Godin has a really good take on this subject. He said that some people are more productive because they are driven by having an instinct to ship instead of an instinct to polish, to be perfect, to justify not shipping.

Well, he is right. **Productivity is all about shipping**, so if you are having trouble with always polishing your work, stop and.

CHAPTER II

HOW TO LEARN

Making pots

I recently heard about an experiment. It was actually a course called "100 Days in the Making": a pottery class.

Students would have the simple task to create beautiful pots from lumps of clay. The catch was that the students were split into two groups.

The first group would be graded on the quality of their best pot, while the second group would be graded based on the number of pots created.

Now the question is: Which group do you think created the best looking, highest quality pot?

Well, by the end of the semester, the second group produced far superior pots, by the simple result of repetition and quantitative experience.

The first group got crippled by perfection and actually delivered sub-par pots. My advice:

Build as many pots as you can!

You see, we notice the same fallacy I mentioned before, and remember:

Shipped is better than perfect

 as Adrian would say.

The quote originates from the early days of Facebook, when Sheryl Sandberg said "Done is better than perfect.".

Always iterate and never settle with nothing because it was not perfect from the first try. We are naturally intelligent adaptive algorithms and we need mistakes to create better products.

Now, I am not saying that failing fast should be a motto for everyone, just build as many pots as you can and you will notice how, over time, you will become really good at building, pots or software, that is.

This applies to programming and also applies to best practices. You can read as much as you want, discuss with 10 specialists, until you start building something, you will not learn enough to actually apply the knowledge.

So, build as much as you possibly can and always iterate to get better versions.

It's simple and it works.

Now the hands-on part: how to learn?

This can be about programming in general, or more about a specific technology or pattern you want to test, depending on your level of experience.

What is clear for me is that a developer should never stop learning. The industry is moving so fast around us that if you stop learning for 1-2 years you kind of miss the train and it is just a matter of time until you will notice your skills are obsolete.

It's harsh, but such is life.

Of course, the principles are the same. A good developer will have no trouble to accommodate in a newer language or platform. Still, the stack is so huge right now that you will need some time to investigate, to **know what you don't know**.

Psychological fatigue is the true productivity killer

Number one requirement for you to learn anything is to have enough energy.

You cannot learn if you are tired or just low on energy. This is the tricky part. You might have time, you might have money and it would still not be enough to learn that new programming language, to tinker with the latest JS framework , etcetera.

The real culprit is the lack of energy, or in other words, **Mental Exhaustion.**

It is hard to solve this and we will discuss it further in the next chapters, for now, get this:

REST before you start learning something new

Take some time off from work, wait for the weekend, ask for dedicated learning time from your manager, etc.

To grow something, you will need both time and energy.

HOW TO LEARN

Programming

This section is dedicated to students, so even if you are a senior developer I would advise to stick around and check how things are for the new generation.

Learning is a fascinating concept. Why do we remember exact scenes from Mr. Robot or Game of Thrones, but we sometimes google "How to do a loop in JavaScript"?

It's all about the human mind and how the brain stores information.

We love stories

We love things that have characters, a setting, a plot, a conflict, a resolution, and are told by someone else.

Remember this as it applies on a subconscious level and can be used for learning new things.

Now, let's discuss about how to approach this in software development.

Great developers never stop learning.

If you hear a lecture and/or read about a topic, you remember about 10%. You can build on that with some demonstrations up to 20%. That would be the maximum retention rate for passive learning.

To go further, you need to be an active participant of the lesson. So, if you have group discussions you can remember more: 50% of the information.

Next steps are practice by doing, where you remember about 75% of what you practice.

In order to learn software development you have to get here (active learning). You need practice in the same way a sports player has to practice, sometimes just to stay in shape.

There is yet another learning method, the most efficient one.

You learn 95% of what you teach others!

If you do a good job at explaining it to someone else, you will definitely remember the shared knowledge.

The principles above are known as the Learning Pyramid, where the worst performant are old-school lectures and the best one is teaching others.

Take it with a grain of salt, as it is not easy to teach others. Give it a try though, and here's my **challenge**:

Write a hello world program in an exotic language like Brainfuck, then teach someone else on how it works so they can write it themselves. The code looks like this:

```
++++++++++[>+++++++>++++++++++>+++>+
<<<<-]>++.>+.+++++++..+++.>++.<<+++++++++++++++.>.
+++.------.--------.>+.>.
```

And the output is:

```
Hello World!
```

Key points in learning software development:

1. Personal projects

Number one on my list are personal projects. This is by far the method with the highest degree of satisfaction and experience. When you work on something that you are passionate about, it just works.

A personal project is something that resonates with you, your hobbies or just something you like. Think about something that will keep you working late at night and will offer you a great deal of accomplishment when you finish something, even if it's a small part.

I will give you an example. In my first year of teaching computer science, the students were given the option to make a small practical application, a standard "library" app, which could account for a part of their grade. The project was already selected and the results were not great, only about 5 students deciding to go ahead and implement it, with mixed results.

For the next year, I proposed a small change in the requirements: the project had to be a personal choice, based on original ideas. Their first task was to find a name for the application, identify the target users and write a short description of the features.

The results were amazing, with over 30 students participating in what became something similar to a small conference, with projects ranging from unique games, dog shelter apps to donation platforms and music editors.

What changed was that the students were working on something they actually liked. Beautiful, right?

So my advice is this: pick something you wanted to do for a long time, find a language/platform you wish to use and go ahead, do it.

It might be something simple, like a Game of Life that I implemented in HTML/JS, or something more complex if you wish.

Yes, it is time consuming, but so is watching Netflix.

2. Online resources

Number two on my list are online resources. Everything you need is already there, online. And usually free. There is no reason to not use the resources and this is equally important also when you are working.

There are thousands of websites and platforms which can be used to learn programming.

For example, a good starting language is python and I would recommend **codecademy.com** for the free course, but there are a lot of other platforms where you can get all the information for free. Think about **w3schools.com**, MIT free courses and so on.

Google is your friend here and actually an important skill. Knowing how to search for information is crucial and can save you a lot of time.

The elephant in the room here is of course, **stackoverflow** which is a good resource when something breaks. Here, I have a single advice:

Don't copy-paste code because you will have "code-spaghetti"
and you will regret it.

3. Find a job

Make a list on LinkedIn with the companies you think are a good
fit, read the online reviews from current and former employees
and send them your CV with a clear message specifying you are
interested in a position on your desired stack.

You will get extra credit for being proactive, which improves
the odds.

*If you really want to be considered, make a short video of
yourself, describing why you want to work with them.*

Mention you read this book, it might help :) Who doesn't want
a 10X developer in their team?

There's always a technical interview.

Prepare for it, you either pass it, or you learn something. If
you fail, ask for advice and work on that. Try again at another
company or the same if you improve.

4. Teaching others

What I mean by teaching others is not necessarily that you
should become a teacher, not by far.

Form working groups with your colleagues when you are preparing or just doing your assignments. People asking other people
how they solved something is the base of stackoverflow's suc-
cess. Use it locally, wisely and it will work very well.

If you are already working and you wish to learn something new, make a short presentation and show it to your team. You will be amazed by how much time consuming it is, but it will help you clear any knowledge gaps you have on the matter.

Make a blog post about the thing you wish to learn. Make a video about it, explaining the concepts to whomever might concern, you will be surprised by the results.

You can then post it on any social media where you are comfortable sharing.

Remember: it does not have to be perfect! Ship and improve!

CHAPTER III

THE ZONE

Valhalla

Those who enter here, will lose track of time

and will be really productive

There are moments in a developer's life when everything just works. You write code, build things, and before you know, it's night time.

I am sure you know exactly what I am talking about here. Those short moments, with bursts of productivity, where everything makes sense.

The Zone is an interesting concept. Easiest analogy that comes into my mind is playing card games.

You could play cards for a whole night, get up and go to work, not being tired at all.

The state is sometimes called "hyperfocus", or "flow".

I called this section Valhalla mostly because this is the state where you want to be.

It usually means you have no distractions, the environment is working smoothly, you understand the requirements and it is only a matter of time until everything will fall into place.

It's really easy for some to enter the zone, and very difficult for others.

I will just mention the standard recommendations that will help you in staying focused:

- Disconnect from anything else

- Avoid micro-distractions

- Take brakes to reduce strain

- Sleep well beforehand

There is one VERY important factor remaining:

If you can keep working in flow for a longer period of time, your productivity will increase tenfold.

So here it is, the most important thing to become a 10X developer is staying in the zone as much as you can.

Easier said than done, right?

The thing about being focused is that you can't quite put your finger on it, find that perfect formula which guarantees that you can enter the zone and stay there until you are done with your task.

Do not look anymore, here are the rules I used and that worked extremely well:

1. Finish all your unfinished business

Remember that electricity bill you forgot to pay and now it pops into your mind every hour or so? Or that call you forgot to make and now it might be a tad too late?

Every unfinished task you have (and most of the time these are personal stuff) becomes a micro-distraction.

We do not realize, but these "leftover" tasks put a great deal of stress on our mindset.

Be honest with yourself

My advice is to be honest with yourself. Think a bit about what is holding you back and solve it before you can really be productive.

Take a few days off and visit that old friend who has been waiting for you for over a year. Wear a mask and keep the social distancing if there is a pandemic around when you read this.

Finish that project you started 6 months ago and something came up.

Send that e-mail that is really important and you are just postponing, etc.

This is pretty easy.

When you do this, starting to clear the backlog or so to speak, you will soon meet some blockage.

Some of these tasks cannot be done. They might just take a very long time or need some specific elements that are simply not at your disposal.

Admit that some things cannot be done and either delegate them or announce that you will not be working on them anymore.

You will soon realize that some of the things were just stressing you out unnecessary, while the reality was they could not be finished anyway.

Admit it and then move along. You just need closure.

If you have a lot of these (personal) backlog items, don't push too hard. Just take them one by one and make sure you either finish them, delegate, or move along.

Each small task that you process will give you enormous relief and will fill you with energy. Check step 2 for how to get even more energy.

2. Get bored

We have a huge problem as a society: We no longer get bored. Think about LinkedIn, Facebook, YouTube, Netflix, Amazon, Twitch, Reddit, 9Gag, Instagram and so on. They all make sure that something interesting can be experienced, a click away.

The human mind is very interesting and we hate being bored. There actually was an experiment where people preferred feeling pain to being bored.

They were put in a simple room, without any kind of digital devices and left alone with their thoughts for 15 minutes.

They were also given the option to press a button and shock themselves if they so desired.

The results were astonishing: 67 percent of men and 25 percent of women chose to inflict pain and pressed the button, getting an electric shock. Wow!

To put it bluntly, get bored! **Put your phone aside, close YouTube and do absolutely nothing!** In 15 minutes you will find work pleasant.

CHAPTER IV

WHO PAYS THE BILL?

Get over the red tape

I will always remember a story that I heard from our mechanic:

A neighbor hired a handyman to make some renovations to their house.

The contractor started the home remodelling and everything went well at first.

After several days, the house owner came back to check on things and noticed some big changes that they did not ask for.

Why did you do this?! asked the owner, feeling his blood pressure rising.

Well, your brother-in-law came and said it would look better this way. I know you said something else, but how should I know on who to listen to? questioned the contractor.

The neighbor was fuming.

You always listen to who is paying! he said.

It's a funny story for me and I chuckle every time I remember it.

I know this is not realistic in our modern work environment. You usually have a team lead, the team lead has a project manager, there is a product owner, a BA and so on.

They discuss with the stakeholders and every time something needs to get done there is this long chain of people who will inadvertently add their own take on how things should be done.

It usually works, just make sure you can detect when the communication channel is not working and find out who is actually the decision-maker and position things so you will get their input.

Otherwise you might just lose time building something for the wrong person.

This is very relevant if you are starting a new project, making proof-of-concepts, prototypes. Make sure the decision-maker is involved otherwise the project might fail without a clear reason on why this happened.

About 70% of the work is understanding people.

What I mean by that is that you need to understand exactly what the problem is or exactly what is desired of the program.

We all get skewed data and modern tools actually made this worse. We need better communication and, most important, with the directly involved stakeholders.

As I said, this is more of a management problem, so maybe as a simple developer you are not that involved in creating specifications.

Remember though you should get your feedback as close to the source as possible.

We need actual contact with our users, see how they are working with our applications and learn from them on how we should improve.

Martin Lindstrom calls this "small data". It is such a refreshing thing to think about small data when all we hear lately is about Big Data and statistics.

Use small data!

Let me tell you an actual example we had on one of our projects:

Our colleague Tudor Nan was having a demo with one of our customers. It was about a mobile application, but being there, he asked one of the users, Mrs. Mariana, how the web application is working, performance wise.

She is one of the kindest people we ever met and always had a good relationship with her.

Her answer took Tudor by surprise. She said the application is very slow, with a sad resigned tone.

Well, this motivated our colleague to start an optimization feature which improved the performance of the app by about 50%.

It was a huge improvement and technical feat and it might have not happened were it for Tudor to not discuss with Mrs. Mariana.

Remember to get your small data from the users!

CHAPTER V

INCREASE THE OUTPUT

Load-bearing functions

Software development is like building houses. You start with a design, create a scaffolding, make the foundation and then you create modules the same way you would add rooms.

In software development, things get better. You can add a whole floor, or control the grains of sand at a molecular level.

You can do anything!

This can quickly turn against you, as you might be tinkering on something small and forget that winter is coming and you have no roof.

This can be solved by good management and experience, yet the danger is always present. You can lose yourself in details and not notice.

In 1974 Donald Knuth published his first volume of "The Art of Computer Programming" and he famously said:

 *Premature optimization is the root of all evil.*

Lets's discuss it a bit.

The full quote sounds like this:

> *Programmers waste enormous amounts of time think-ing about, or worrying about, the speed of noncritical parts of their programs, and these attempts at efficiency actually have a strong negative impact when debugging and maintenance are considered. We should forget about small efficiencies, say about 97% of the time: premature optimization is the root of all evil. Yet we should not pass up our opportunities in that critical 3%.*

You see, nobody mentions the last part. You have to be careful on not wasting time with non-critical parts, yet you should keep an eye on those 3% opportunities which can have an amazing impact on your application.

We have an inside joke inside our team. When you are working on a service and you notice that it is used in several (10+) criti-cal places, we call those "load bearing functions". Basically it is the same idea with a load bearing wall. You can knock some walls out to make a room larger, but if you do this with a load bearing wall, the whole structure will come down.

Focus on this functions. Write unit tests, optimize them and treat them well in general.

Spend time here and write them as modular as you can, so you have flexibility when things will inevitably change in the future.

Imagine this: you have built the house, and then you need an-other floor, between two existing ones. Almost impossible right?

Not if you used containers and a good support structure!

Check out **functional programming** for more on this.

CHAPTER VI

STAY HUMBLE

Kindness

I was really inspired by Justin Kan and I noticed that he often uses the expression *"be kind to others", and*

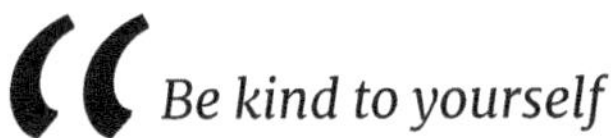

Be kind to yourself

Powerful! Yet I do not know if you should start with yourself, start with others or both.

Most likely you will have to start with yourself, we usually put so much pressure and expectations on ourselves.

And we forget to be kind. We forget that it is normal to have limits. We forget that it is normal to make mistakes.

We are surrounded by pressure, stressful environments, and of course, the pandemic does not make things easier.

Now, let us move forward, being kind to others. I am quite sure you have heard about soft skills. They are crucial for a good developer and perhaps for everyone involved in the so-called modern workforce.

We need both soft skills and technical skills to really grow and bring value in your team.

Being kind to others usually requires empathy. That is my favorite soft skill. Having empathy means that you understand why people behave the way they do, and this helps you help them.

Of course, kindness is so much more. We associate kindness with being friendly, generous, and considerate. Truth is, kindness, after a certain point in life requires courage and strength.

Once you become a proficient developer, and perhaps build a successful tech product, it is easy to become arrogant and insensitive to others. Do not go there, as you will only find hubris at the end of the path.

In our industry, there are several types of so-called developers. We have already discussed about the 10X, the productive developer.

You most likely heard about rockstar developers, unicorns, ninja, gurus, magicians, and all kind of silly names.

I will focus a bit on the rockstar concept.

It is interesting. So, in my opinion, a rockstar developer is kind of dangerous, for a startup and a company in general. What usually happens is, they become a critical part of the project.

And if anything were to happen, it is another project that will simply fail. They become load bearing themselves. And this is the tricky part, where every developer should make sure that the application, the system and the code will work even if we are not around.

Don't make yourself indispensable

This is unnatural for most developers because we always try to find a way to integrate ourselves in a project. Remember that at one point the code will be maintained by someone else.

So, it is almost the same as in a business. You must be careful and not get attached to your code.

Regarding rockstars, it is rare to have more than one in a project, they usually do not get along with other hyper-productive developers.

Still, do not underestimate the value rockstar developers can bring in a team. If the stars align, they can take your application to the moon.

Now, let us move forward: the genius programmer. I sometimes chuckle when I hear the term, the genius programmer is different.

It is similar with the other productive types of developers, but lacks the necessary soft skills to integrate with a team. So, what happens is, they usually have a big ego and will not accept any kind of criticism.

They might even subtract from more menial work, like writing unit tests, refactoring or writing comments because they find it below their level.

Sometimes these developers are really good at specific tasks and completely lacking at others. For example, being really good with technical skills and a complete lack of soft skills.

This can be managed, but usually what happens is they create a toxic environment within their teams. They are extremely productive, the caveat being that they usually work alone.

Another productive type of developers are the glass cannons. The term originates from gaming and it refers to a character class that has remarkable offensive power, but has low defense.

The thing here is that developers that fit in this category are extremely productive, until one day when they aren't.

Sometimes the culprit is burnout because they push themselves too hard, or something else, the important part here is that we should all support our colleagues and make the best we can to avoid big hits in morale and productivity.

Actually this is the only reason I brought up these specific typologies. It is very easy on your way to 10X development to fall in one of these traps, where your efficiency might actually have a negative impact on the team and inevitably on the product.

Here is my advice:

Work in a team or at least find a work buddy. Someone who is near you and you can ask questions, or just be there. It helps, a lot.

Will Smith recently said this:

> *If you can't beat the fear, just do it scared*

He's right!

Fear means that you are outside of you comfort zone, and this means you are moving forward.

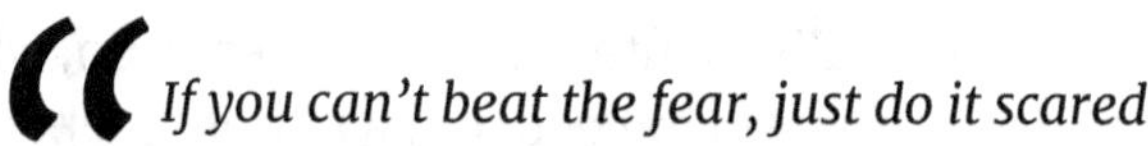

So move forward and don't forget to be kind!

CHAPTER VII

BURNOUT

A robot story

A few years ago, a group of scientists were training some small robots to navigate in a room.

They had this floor and the logic was quite simple: if a robot would hit a wall or another robot, it would get penalty points, otherwise bonus points.

In a nutshell, they were training the robots to avoid obstacles.

The algorithm worked and soon enough, most of the robots were moving around, avoiding obstacles and each other.

Sometimes there would be bumps, but the algorithm would adapt and the units would move again.

During the experiments, one of the robots was not that lucky.

It has bumped so many times against obstacles, had so many negative feedbacks, that after a while **it just stopped moving**.

That is burnout!

A study revealed some stages where we can recognize the problems before they become to large to handle.

The first stage is **the honeymoon effect**, where you try as hard as possible to prove yourself on the new project or job. This stage might be connected with the so-called "Impostor syndrom".

Here I would advice to just take things as they come and have honest discussions about what you can and cannot do.

The second phase is the **onset of stress**.

You realize some days are more difficult than others and anxiety with fatigue start to affect you directly.

Your productivity lowers, you have trouble focusing on the current tasks, etc.

This is the stage where the poor robot was bumping into things.

The solution is quite simple, once you understand what is happening:

Look for the reset button.

Ask for a few days off, or even better, ask for help from one of your colleagues. Shared responsibility reduces stress. A lot.

If you do nothing to fix this, the third stage is **chronic stress**.

You will feel exhausted and might even have panic attacks. Apathy or even anger are common at this point. You do not want to be here. Ask for medical help at this point.

The next level is actual **burnout**. At this stage you feel empty inside, self-doubt and look for social isolation. You might even become physically ill.

In this stage you can no longer continue as usual and intervention is paramount.

You will feel obsessed with work and life problems and have a pessimistic view about the world.

If you are here, it is time to take a break.

It's a marathon, not a sprint

That is what George would say to our junior colleagues. Everyone is giving 110% when they start working as developers and it is easy to forget that the issues will still be there the next day so working overtime will not solve the problem, it will just make you tired.

We have strict no overtime policy, and it still happens sometime, so we spend time monitoring how each member of the team is doing, just to make sure they do not overwork themselves.

You see, the Zone is a double edge sword. You might be in the flow at 6 PM and solve in that hour more that you solved an entire day.

Still, we advise to come an hour late the next morning or just take a day off to rest.

Otherwise, a burnout might take you out of action for a week or even months.

The impact is also huge when you graduate and start working full 8 hours per day as a developer. Everyone comes close to burnout in the first months, then slowly realize that George is right, it's a marathon, not a sprint.

Once we accept that, we can discuss about **work-life balance**.

CHAPTER VIII

DISCUSSION

About the HOW

I have discussed about these topics to hundreds of students during my activity as a teacher.

Some of them graduated and now work as developers for renowned companies like Microsoft, Google or NTT.

Some became entrepreneurs and started software development companies or even created startups for their own product. Some of them graduated and now work alongside our own team.

Some of them gave up on programming and now do something else.

They all make me proud !

My simple 5 words advice on how to improve things sounds like this:

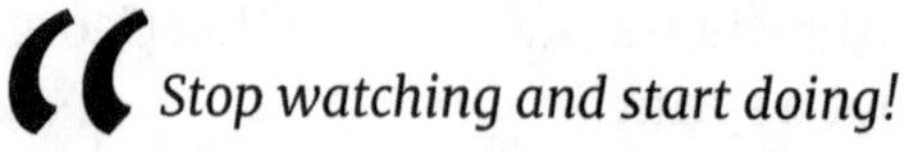 *Stop watching and start doing!*

Sometimes we trick ourselves to think that we are doing something, when we read books, articles and watch tutorials.

We don't. Remember the pot example. We need to ship things to the world for us to truly learn something new.

Here is our CodexWorks manifesto:

You can do anything!

If you put time and energy in something, it grows.

So keep doing it!

Do things that make you proud.

You are changing the world, one bit at a time!

George would argue that perhaps they are just words written to generate hype, and he would be absolutely right.

On the other hand, I guess that is how a manifesto is supposed to work.

I learned that human beings need hype in their life.

These words mean a lot to me and I hope they will motivate you to make an extra step today, an extra step tomorrow, so in the end you will be further down the path of your true potential.

RANDOM THOUGHTS

While writing on this software booklet I took a few notes and realized that it would be a shame to discard them away, so I will add these sections in which I will open new topics or provide more details on some of the chapters.

*Why the h**l were old games so hard?*

Why were games in the 90's so difficult? You would make a single mistake and you had to start over.

Now, most games have checkpoints, saves and most of them are incredibly easy to play.

Someone said that back then we had enough free time and free mind to enjoy something like that. I agree.

There seems to be a technical and a human component in the long answer. First, saving games was not possible until later in game development, notably The Legend of Zelda being the first game to include a battery-backed memory on the game cartridge itself.

Later games continued to use the style of the arcade machines and those older games, mainly because it was easier to program that way.

The second reason is the part about not having enough free mind.

We are no longer bored and only a really small number of games like Dark Souls, Flappy Bird etc survived.

There is a simple solution to this problem.

A few months ago I participated to an online workshop organized by Martin Lindstrom. For me, Martin "owns" the word branding and I learned a lot from him.

One thing that took us by surprise was the moment Martin showed us his smartphone. It was black and it took us a few moments to realize it was a simple block of wood, painted black.

He had no phone!

The reason for this choice was the huge improvement in productivity and energy that the lack of a mobile phone created.

Interesting!

I now give his advice to everyone. Life happens once you put down the mobile phone. Try it!

What made me write this book?

When I was younger I remember reading a book about program-ming. It was a special book, dedicated to students preparing for the computer science olympiad.

It motivated me.

I liked how the authors found a way to present a scary subject in a friendly way.

I still remember that book and I felt that maybe it would help others if I wrote one too.

Also, when George and I were in high school, we somehow managed to install Macromedia Flash on a computer.

We painfully worked for about a day and at the end we managed to make the wheels on a wagon, spin.

The exported video with the animation was about 20 seconds long and occupied about 20 GB. **We felt on top of the world!**

I still get that feeling when I build something and it works, so writing this booklet feels like a natural way for me to give back.

Fast forward a bit and I was winning first place at a national contest on applied computer science.

Were it not for those ugly spinning wheels, I might not have reached that level.

Celebrate your wins, no matter how small!

How to start when you feel overwhelmed?

Two weeks ago I saw a video from Justin Kan and he explained how he deals with complex tasks. He said to break everything in atomic pieces until you can do something, then get momentum based on that.

It makes sense!

Break complex tasks in smaller units

One of the mistakes I often see with my students is that they begin an application with the packages, then start writing the models, then the controllers, the services etc.

When everything is done, a few hours later, they hit Run and expect it to work.

I can predict with about 99% accuracy that it won't.

It never runs on the first try.

Things can be complicated even further.

They can spend the following 2-3 days trying to fix about 100 errors or bugs.

Start small and add code on the way up.

Always start with the classic *Hello World*. Does it build? Perfect! This means that you now have the environment right.

Do you need a GUI? Render a single button with the text "It works".

Do you know how time consuming it is to hit Run after 5 hours just to see that you have the wrong dependency and the error message is spread on several pages? Not to mention the drain it has on your morale as a developer.

Start small and build on the way up. Treat every roadblock as a single element and make sure that each module is doing one thing well. Then you build the other modules, in the same way.

Then you make them talk to each other, ideally adding one by one in the mix, so the cake won't blow up.

With practice, it will work on the first try.

I had a great teacher when I was doing prep work for the Computer Science Olympics.

One of the things that I was most impressed of was when he would write a program in C++, press run and it worked on the first try. **Whoah!**

At that point, we (the students) were having compiler error or infinite loops every 10 lines.

I looked up to that skill and wondered if I would ever reach that level of technical proficiency. Several years later I did and then it was my turn to teach a new generation of developers.

I always remember him when I press run and it just works. So Horatiu Cristurean, thank you!

There is one point to consider though. This is exactly like a muscle. You have to be there, writing code every week, otherwise you will lose some of your hard-earned skills.

What to do when you feel overwhelmed?

Ask yourself these questions:

· How will this affect my life tomorrow?

· How will this affect my life next month?

· How will this affect my life next year?

· How will this affect my life in 10 years?

That's it. You will quickly learn that most stress comes from things that won't even matter next month and most certainly you won't remember next year.

This helps you sift through the really important ones and prioritize your energy on things that truly matter.

After you have a clear mind and assessed the importance of the said thing you can begin to work for a solution. Step by step, find the best course of actions to solve any problem you may encounter. Repeat as many times as necessary.

As an observation, it always is about people. You won't have issues when dealing with a computer. A computer won't make you feel that you have a responsibility or that you will be held accountable.

If you have a deadline for example, the pressure is not from your calendar app, the pressure is from the people waiting for you to finish on time and their reaction if you don't. Simple!

How to get more energy?

I learned a lot from Colin Whitfield and his lessons stayed with me for a long time. The first thing that worked for me, energy wise, was delegation. I tried to do everything and most of the time I was a bottleneck for our team.

So I learned to delegate and prioritize.

We also learned this term: Courageous Imperfect Action, or CIA. It is another way to say done is better than perfect and it allowed us to take decisions fast.

I remember one of the exercises we did during our training:

In the morning, stay in bed or somewhere peaceful for 30 min and think:

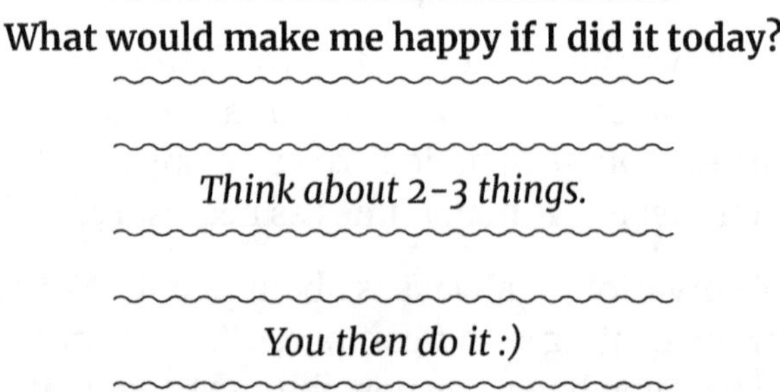

You'll soon notice there are lots of small stuff which you will love and once you start doing those, your energy level will increase a lot. You will start being productive again.

Simple works!

THANK YOU!

Acknowledgment: Thank you CodexWorks Technologies and Babeș–Bolyai University for providing the opportunity to expand my knowledge.

Follow me on Linkedin!

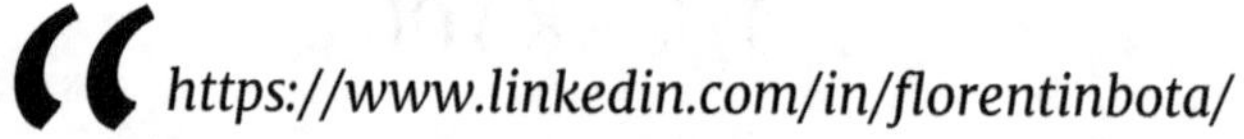 *https://www.linkedin.com/in/florentinbota/*

My favorite topics are

- Software

- AI

- Teaching

SoftwareBooklet.com

www.ingramcontent.com/pod-product-compliance
Lightning Source LLC
Chambersburg PA
CBHW060918130726
48001CB00006B/2301